AGAINS T ALL ODDS

FROM THE GRIT OF JAMAICA TO THE GRIT AND GLORY OF CANADA

Published by Howill Nation Publishing

Dallas, Texas, USA

publishing@howillnation.com

Cover design, interior layout, and production by Howill Nation Publishing.

Library of Congress Control Number (LCCN): Available upon request.

ISBN (Print):978-1-7369937-3-6 ISBN (eBook): 978-1-7369937-3-7

Printed in the United States of America

First Edition: June 2025

For permissions, inquiries, or speaking engagements, visit: normanhamilton.com

The Man Behind the Story

Before the first step was taken,

Before the papers were stamped,

Before the snow, the setbacks, the sacrifice— There was a boy from Spoilers.

And that boy became a man who refused to break.

This is Norman Hamilton. Immigrant. Father. Fighter. Builder.

He didn't inherit success—he built it from scratch, with nothing but grit in his gut and fire in his faith.

This story isn't just about survival. It's about becoming.

It's about the quiet strength behind every loud breakthrough. The spirit behind every hard-earned win.

The man behind the movement.

Look closely.

This isn't just a face. It's a map.

A living testament that against all odds, legacy is still possible.

For the One Who Rose

To the boy who sold juice in Spoilers,

who walked straight through gunfire and never blinked.

To the young man who slept on floors, shoveled snow, and gave blood to pay tuition.

To the dreamer they doubted— but who rose anyway.

This is for you, Norman.

You didn't wait for a handout.

You built your life—against all odds.

— N.H.

FOREWORD
BY JUDAH WILLIAM

The first time I met Norman Hamilton, I didn't just meet a man—I met a storm. A quiet storm. The kind that doesn't show off, but shifts everything it touches.

Norman is the embodiment of what it means to be built from nothing. He didn't have a blueprint. He was the blueprint. Born in the heat of Kingston, raised by a single mother with more hope than resources, Norman started hustling at seven—not because it was trendy, but because survival demanded it. From pushing snow in sub-zero Canada to giving blood to pay tuition, this man has paid his dues in pain and persistence.

I've watched him navigate the streets of Spoilers and the boardrooms of North America with the same energy—bold, unshaken, and full of faith. He's been handcuffed, gunned down, frozen, fired, and robbed. Yet here he stands—unbroken, undefeated, unashamed.

This book is not just a story. It's a mirror for anyone who's ever

wondered, "Can I rise from where I am?"

Yes. You can. Norman did. And through these pages, he hands you his scars as proof.

Against All Odds

Against All Odds is more than a memoir. It's a manual for the misjudged, a map for the misunderstood, and a movement for those who've been counted out.

Read it slow. Let it sink. Then rise.

— Judah Williams

Mentor. Visionary. Brother.

Table of Contents

CHAPTER ONE

BORN FOR THE BATTLE

St. Thomas-born. Home-delivered. Raised by a warrior: Mama.

Some children are welcomed into the world with bright hospital lights, soft cotton blankets, and a team of professionals standing by. I entered this life in a one-room house tucked in the rugged stretch of St. Thomas, Jamaica. No nurse. No doctor. No sterile tools. Just the raw determination of my mother, a woman who had already lost count of how many tears she'd cried, and the thick, invisible hand of God. My birth wasn't announced with balloons or photographs—it was marked by grit, groaning, and grace. There was no luxury. Just the earth beneath us, and the heavens watching over. That kind of entrance into life doesn't leave you neutral. It brands you. From the moment I drew my first breath, I was introduced to struggle. And whether I liked it

or not, struggle became my first classroom.

My mother was already a seasoned soldier by the time I came into the world. She had given birth to one child, and carried more weight than any woman should ever have to. We didn't have enough—never did. Not enough food. Not enough sleep. Not enough space. But there was always just enough love to go

around, and somehow, even more strength. Mama never sat us down and explained how tired she was. She didn't complain. But you could see it—the quiet fatigue in her eyes, the way her shoulders curved with invisible burdens. She didn't need to say she was hungry; you just noticed she always ate last. That kind of silent sacrifice does something to a boy. I watched her carefully, not just as a son, but as a student. Every time she got back up after being knocked down by life, I took mental notes. Her perseverance was louder than any sermon I'd ever hear.

By the time I was ten, I wasn't just a child anymore—I was a contributor. While other boys played football in the street or ran through mango groves chasing laughter, I was working. I sold banana chips on the roadside. I offered rides to older students walking to high school. I partnered with a vendor on the weekends who sold clothes at the market. And not once did I spend that money on myself. I didn't care about toys or new shoes. Every dollar I earned was my attempt at giving Mama a break. I wanted her to sleep without worry, to breathe without that constant tightness in her chest. I didn't know how to say it then, but I was doing what boys become men by doing—I was choosing responsibility over comfort.

Life in St. Thomas was no fairy tale. It was a furnace—one that forged resilience. We didn't sit around waiting for help. That mindset didn't exist. I learned early that life wasn't fair, but it could be fought for. We stretched every coin. I learned to negotiate at a young age. I knew the value of work, not because someone taught me in school, but because we lived it—every day, every hour. Laziness wasn't just frowned upon; it could kill

your future. My mother ran that household like a military base disguised as a home, and I—like my sibling—learned how to endure without applause, how to win with little.

But no amount of hustle prepared me for the blow that came

just as I was entering my tenth year of life. One morning, a phone call shattered our world. My father had been shot and killed. The details were blurry. The pain was not. The shock moved through our house like a thief in the night. No time to prepare. No moment to process. He was gone. Just like that. In one conversation, I stopped being a child and started becoming something else—something older, something sharper, something I wasn't ready to be. That loss rewired me.

Grief hit our household like a storm that refused to pass. Mama didn't fall apart. But something in her spirit folded quietly. She became even more focused, even more determined, even more guarded. My siblings changed too—some withdrew, others toughened. As for me, I had to grow up with no blueprint for what a father should be, only a burning desire to not let this pain define me. I began to understand something most kids my age didn't: life doesn't wait for you to catch up. Either you rise, or you drown.

I promised myself that day—I would not be a victim. I would not live as a statistic. I would find a way to turn this tragedy into fuel. And so, I worked harder. Hustled smarter. And when I made my first big earnings—forty thousand Jamaican dollars from selling juice on the hot streets of Kingston—it wasn't a selfish celebration. It was sacred. That cash represented every early morning, every burned hand from boiling bottles, every

"no" turned into a "maybe" on the grind. I placed that money in Mama's hand like it was a medal. She looked at me, and for the first time in a long time, I saw joy break through her tired eyes. Then came the tears—not the usual ones from frustration or fatigue, but tears of honor, of pride. I had done something. I had become someone. I wasn't just helping pay bills—I was building a bridge to her next chapter.

That bridge took flight—literally. She used part of that money to purchase her first airplane ticket. Destination: the Bahamas. She had secured work there. It wasn't glamorous, but it was an opportunity. That trip wasn't just a change in scenery—it was a change in destiny. Watching her walk toward that airport gate, knowing I had helped make that possible, was the first time I ever felt what manhood tasted like. That money had opened a door. That door had unlocked hope. And hope, in our world, was more valuable than gold.

Mama was my foundation. Her silence was louder than any lecture. Her prayers were more powerful than any professor's advice. She didn't just raise us—she built us. I am who I am today because of her unseen sacrifices, her unspoken strength, her unrelenting faith. She invested in me without asking for returns. She bet on me before I had proof. And now, everything I create—every home, every hustle, every business—is a thank you letter to her written in bricks, sweat, and legacy.

When people ask me, "Norman, how did you do it?" I don't start with degrees or resumes. I don't talk about business plans. I talk about her. I talk about that patched-up house in St. Thomas, the leaky zinc roof, the smell of boiled dumplings, the mornings we

walked miles to school, and the woman who carried us all with fire in her chest and no room for fear.

This chapter isn't a story about lack. It's a declaration of legacy. It's not a tale of poverty—it's a testimony of power. Because power isn't what you're given—it's what you build when life hands you bricks made of pain. I didn't come from ease—I came from endurance. I wasn't birthed in comfort—I was carved out of chaos.

And if I—Norman Hamilton, barefoot boy from St. Thomas— can rise from grief, hustle past odds, and build something from the ashes of a fatherless childhood, then trust me… you can rise too. No matter what battle you were born into, you were born to win it. You weren't made to break. You were made to build.

You were made for more.

CHAPTER TWO

HER TEARS LIT MY FIRE

"Mama cried. Norman rose. This is where resilience was born."
"Some women carry babies. My mother carried nations."
– Norman Hamilton

They say tears are weakness. But I learned early—some tears are strategy. Some tears are strength disguised as surrender. I saw it that day when I handed my mother the first stack of money I had ever truly earned—forty thousand Jamaican dollars. It wasn't a fortune to the world, but in our world, it was everything. It was sweat turned into currency. It was the sun on my back, the dust in my lungs, the rejection from people who turned their noses up at a little boy selling juice on corners. It

was my grind on paper.

When I placed that money in her hands, she didn't speak. Not immediately. She looked down at it like it was foreign—like it didn't belong in her world of stretch and scrape. Then she looked at me, and her lips trembled. Slowly, silently, the tears came. But they weren't the tears I had seen before—the tired kind that slipped out when the rice ran out or when the landlord knocked too hard. These were different. These were full of meaning,

memory, and maybe even a little bit of relief. For the first time in a long time, Mama cried not because of what we lacked—but because of what we had become.

That moment was a turning point in my life. I didn't feel

like a boy anymore. I felt like a man. A man who had finally lifted, even if only for a moment, the mountain that had lived on my mother's back since the day I was born. Her tears were my ceremony. That was the day I crossed into purpose—not because I had arrived, but because I had become useful. I had become an answer to the same prayers she had whispered into the zinc roof on nights when hunger kept us all awake.

You see, my mother didn't just raise children—she waged war against a system that told her she would never win. She fought with silence, with prayer, with pots that boiled more water than food. She stitched our school uniforms with tired fingers. She made one cup of rice stretch for eight people. She kept the light on in the house not with electricity, but with faith. No husband. No partner. Just grit and God. And now, she held the proof in her hand—that her sacrifice was not in vain. That her seed had started to bloom.

She didn't use the entire forty thousand. In her usual way, she tucked some of it aside, probably thinking of the next rent, the next set of school books, the next emergency. But with a portion of it, she bought something for herself. Something she had never done before. She bought a plane ticket—to the Bahamas. Her first flight. Her first time leaving Jamaica. She wasn't going on vacation. She wasn't sightseeing. She was going to work. To start over. To take another swing at life, this time in a different place. And I—we—had made that possible.

Watching her prepare for that flight was something I'll never forget. The night before she left, she sat in the living room with her Bible on her lap, her fingers tracing the pages like they held the map to her future. There was no fanfare. No Instagram post. No send-off party. Just quiet resolve and a mother on a mission. She ironed her clothes like they were armor. She braided her hair like it was a crown. And when she hugged me before leaving, she said only this: "Mi son… don't forget where you come from."

That sentence became a tattoo on my soul.

I carried that sentence—and her spirit—everywhere I went to Humber College and York University in Canada. here I sat in lecture halls knowing I didn't belong but determined to prove I did. To the aisles of Walmart, where I stocked shelves through the night, whispering prayers under my breath just to stay awake. To the early days of entrepreneurship, when my bank account said no but my calling said go. And even now, in boardrooms and meetings, her voice is there. Her lessons echo. Her example leads.

Because the truth is—I wasn't built by wealth. I was built by watching a woman walk through fire and come out clothed in dignity. I wasn't shaped by comfort. I was shaped by kitchens that held more prayer than food, and mornings that started with nothing but ended with something. She taught me how to give my last without showing it. How to lead without shouting. How to bend without breaking. She taught me that strength isn't loud—it's consistent.

People see resilience as a trending word. A nice quote to share. But I lived it. Resilience is watching your mother walk five miles to a job that barely pays and still return with bread and a smile. Resilience is hearing her pray your name into heaven while she battles hell on earth. Resilience is waking up every day in a broken house with an unbroken spirit. It's forty thousand Jamaican dollars placed in the hands that once wiped your nose and now wipe away tears of triumph.

My mother's tears lit a fire in me. Not because she cried—

but because of what those tears represented. Release. Reward. A revolution in the making. I saw in her eyes that day what it meant to build something out of nothing. And I made a decision. I would not waste her sacrifice. I would not let her legacy drown in my comfort. I would multiply what she started.

Every boy she birthed, every scar she covered, every door she opened with her bare hands—I would turn them into chapters in a bigger story. A story of rising. Of breaking cycles. Of becoming more than what the world expected from a barefoot boy in St. Thomas.

Mama, this chapter is for you. For your fight. For your faith. For your fire. For every time you cried in silence and still got up to make breakfast. For every time you patched our clothes while your heart was breaking. For every prayer you prayed without ever seeing the answer—until now.

You didn't just raise a son. You raised a fire.

And now the world will feel its heat.

CHAPTER THREE

SPOILERS IF SURVIVA L

"Street smarts, survival codes, and childhood in a combat zone."
"The ghetto doesn't just test you—it teaches you. If you live through it,
you earn your degree in survival."
– Norman Hamilton

If you've never lived in a place like Spoilers, it's hard to explain what waking up really meant. You didn't just open your eyes— you braced your soul. Every morning was a gamble. You got up not because the day was promising, but because surrender wasn't an option. Spoilers wasn't just a Kingston neighborhood—it was a war zone that dressed itself in denim and reggae. On the surface, there was rhythm: sound systems blasting from corner shops, men playing dominoes under zinc roofs, barefoot kids chasing deflated footballs. But beneath all that sound and sunshine was a

simmering tension that never slept.

You learned to read the street like a language. You could feel when something was off by the way the wind shifted, or how fast the birds flew past the rooftops. Laughter could flip into screaming in seconds. A harmless street argument could turn into a bloodstain by nightfall. And if you didn't learn to decode

the rhythm of danger, the streets would write your obituary

before your dreams ever stood a chance.

I wasn't raised in violence—but I was baptized in it. It was in the air, in the body language of men who never smiled too long, in the silent stare of boys who had seen one too many good ones get taken out. Spoilers didn't give you warnings. You either adapted, disappeared—or died. Reputation ran deeper than the law. Loyalty could cost you your life. And every alley, every corner, every creaky gate came with its own unwritten code. To survive, you had to observe fast, move sharp, and never, ever forget who was watching.

That's where I earned my first degree—long before any college called my name. I learned emotional intelligence, not in a classroom, but from watching men switch moods like weapons. I learned timing—not on a clock—but by knowing when to speak and when silence could save your life. I learned that fear, if you didn't master it, would eat your confidence alive. And confidence? That wasn't optional in Spoilers. Confidence was survival.

During my years at Kingston Technical, life was a balancing act between ambition and adversity. I didn't just walk to school—I marched through a minefield. Most mornings, I'd wake before the sun, grab my bucket of juice, and head downtown. I wasn't just hustling to make lunch money—I was learning the mechanics of commerce, customer service, rejection, and resilience, all before 8 a.m. Every sale was a victory. Every "no" was a lesson. And every coin I earned carried the scent of struggle and the sound of Mama's prayers.

Downtown Kingston—Big Tree, Parade, was a beast of its own. Crowded. Loud. Alive. But also dangerous. One day, while working my regular route, I saw a car pull up fast. No plates. No greetings. Just a man with a cold stare and a loaded question:

"Gimme di phone."

I froze. Then handed it over. But something inside me snapped. Not out of pride—but out of principle. I chased the car. No weapon. No plan. Just the fire of a boy tired of being prey. It wasn't about the phone. It was about dignity. About sending a message—to the street and to myself: I might bend, but I don't bow.

Spoilers taught me that.

In Spoilers, we walked in the middle of the road. That wasn't just a route—it was a statement. Sidewalks were for strangers. The middle? That was for those who belonged. The middle said, "I know these streets." The middle said, "I see you—but I'm not scared of you." That walk taught me posture. That posture taught me presence. And that presence? It follows me into boardrooms to this day.

But even in the chaos, angels showed up. The Baptist church around the corner became more than a building—it became a bridge. They saw a future in me that I hadn't yet dared to imagine.

Across the street, in the Central Police Station, more unlikely angels stood guard. Inspector Ms. Row and Sergeant Bennett made sure I had food during lunch breaks. No handouts—just honor. They never announced it. Never posted it. They just did

it. Consistently. Quietly. Powerfully. And their kindness rewrote part of my story.

Then came an older man around the corner of Wildman Street. and full of quiet fire. One day, he looked me in the eye and said,

“Young man, you’ve got more in you. You will be rich. Focus on your future.”

Those words hit me like prophecy. I slowed the hustle. Turned my focus to Kingston Technical. That school didn’t just give me tools—it gave me belief. It taught me that my hands could build things greater than struggle. That the same hands that carried juice buckets could one day carry blueprints, contracts, legacies.

Spoilers didn’t just shape me. It introduced me to my brothers— Demar and Dalton. We weren’t blood, but we were bonded by fire. Demar could laugh in the middle of a storm. Dalton could spot a liar from a mile away. We didn’t talk about our pain—but we recognized it in each other’s silence. We survived Spoilers together. And years later, we found ourselves in Canada—new soil, same roots. Same fire.

In Toronto, people couldn’t understand us fully. How could they? They hadn’t walked where we walked. But we laughed at the same old memories. We sharpened each other. We reminded each other who we were before immigration papers and credit scores.

I wasn’t chasing popularity back then. I was chasing peace. Peace from poverty. Peace from shame. Peace from the street’s grip on my potential. Spoilers gave me scars, yes—but it gave me structure. And those principles still follow me:

Never walk in fear.

Show up present, even if you feel invisible. Protect your name.

Guard your energy. Hustle with honor.

And when the heat rises—walk in the middle of the road.

So no—I don't walk into rooms needing validation. I walk in with Spoilers in my spine. Every conference. Every keynote. Every platform. You're not just hearing a man—you're hearing the resilience of a community that refused to let me die. A community that raised me with prayer, police lunches, and God's protection in the middle of madness.

I carry them. I carry every man I saw fall. Every woman who cooked with nothing but hope. Every child who didn't make it out. I carry every street, every smell, every gunshot that whispered, "You might be next." I carry the message that where you come from doesn't have to be where you end.

Spoilers tried to bury me. But it only planted me.

And now—I bloom.

CHAPTER FOUR

MIDDLE OF THE ROAD – STRATEGY OR SURVI VAL

Why walking in the center of the street could mean life or death.
"Never walk on the side. In life—just like in Kingston—walk in the middle. Walk bold. Walk like you belong."
– Norman Hamilton

They say life teaches you in classrooms, with chalkboards and calm explanations. But growing up in the community of Spoilers, Kingston, Jamaica, life teaches you in motion. In noise. In fear. In the flicker between calm and chaos. There were no textbooks, no well-lit whiteboards, no bells to mark the next period. There was just movement, instinct, and the unrelenting weight of survival. You didn't sit and take notes. You moved and took cover. There, survival wasn't abstract—it was intimate. It was spiritual. It was

sacred.

One lesson stood out from all the rest, a quiet instruction that marked me for life:

Walk in the middle of the road.

To outsiders, that might sound like a metaphor. Maybe even poetic. But to me, it was literal. It was tactical. It was a survival code passed down not by elders, but by the streets themselves. You don't learn that kind of wisdom in a sermon. You learn it through heat. Through pressure. Through the split-second decisions that determine whether you go home or become another mural on a zinc fence.

I remember the day I truly understood the meaning of walking in the middle. Kingston was boiling. The streets were buzzing with life, but the kind of life that hides a death wish under every smile. That day, I was downtown—somewhere between Parade and Jubilee Market—carrying my juice buckets like usual. I was grinding. Not for fun, not for school fees, but because Mama needed bread on the table and the gas meter didn't care that I was just a teenager. Hustle wasn't optional. It was my contribution to our survival.

Duke Street was a familiar battlefield: vendors yelling, barefoot children darting through honking cars, sound systems shaking walls that had seen better days. But even in all that noise, I felt it. That silence. The kind of eerie stillness that creeps in just before something breaks. It's a silence the street teaches you to recognize—like the moment just before lightning splits the sky.

That's when I saw them. Two men. No words. No greetings. Just steady steps and too-quiet eyes. Something in me locked up. The buckets felt heavier. My breath tightened. I knew.

Then it happened.

One of them stepped forward, pulled a gun, and leveled it right at me.

"Yow, youth—run di phone."

Just like that. No raised voice. No wild threats. Just command.

I froze—not because I was weak, but because my mind was doing math at a million miles an hour. I was measuring the cost of pride against the price of purpose. I had to choose: dignity or life? Pride or future? I had maybe two seconds to decide whether I was going to be stubborn or still breathing.

I handed the phone over.

They disappeared into a waiting car. Most people would call that the end. But for me, it wasn't over. Not by a long shot. Something in me snapped—not in anger, but in defiance. I ran after the car. No weapon. No plan. No backup. Just my bare feet and a fire in my chest.

It wasn't about the phone. It wasn't even about revenge. It was about sending a message to myself and to the street: I don't disaąąear. I don't fold. I may lose a moment, but I don't lose me.

That day, something sacred clicked inside me. Walk in the middle of the road.

In Spoilers, we literally walked in the middle. Not on the sidewalk. Not close to the curb. The sidewalk was where tourists and targets walked. But the middle? That's where the statement was made. It was defiance. It was identity. It was presence. You didn't need to say anything. You just had to move like you weren't

afraid to be seen. Like you were born for the heat, not hiding from it.

When you walked in the middle, you told the block, I'm from here. I belong. I know the code. Even the danger respected that posture. It didn't guarantee safety, but it gave you space. And in a place where space was the difference between life and legacy, that mattered.

Over time, walking in the middle became more than

physical— it became mental. It became spiritual. I wasn't just walking on streets—I was walking through stages of manhood. Every step forward was a rejection of fear and a declaration of identity. I was becoming more than just a hustler. I was becoming rooted. Unshakeable.

I carried that posture all the way to Canada.

I remember my first winter in Toronto. Everything was unfamiliar—cold, distant, organized in a way that felt almost sterile compared to the rawness of Kingston. But even then, I remembered: Walk in the middle. That meant owning my space in a boardroom even when I was the only immigrant in the room. That meant pitching myself for contracts when I barely had a portfolio. That meant walking into spaces where my accent made heads turn—but still speaking with clarity, conviction, and calm.

Because once you've walked with a gun in your face, no man's title can intimidate you.

Spoilers gave me more than scars. It gave me strategy. That middle-of-the-road mentality became a framework for life:

In relationships, don't play the sidelines. Be honest. Be present. Walk in the middle.

In business, don't whisper your value. Move with clarity. Walk in the middle.

In fatherhood, don't just show up for birthdays. Show up for discipline, for dreams, for direction. Walk in the middle.

Even now, I pass that same code to my son. Not just about sidewalks and streets—but about life. I tell him: Don't shrink. Don't tiątoe around your ąurąose. Walk like your name means something. Walk like the sąace is already yours—even if you have to earn it every day.

Because walking in the middle is not about arrogance. It's about alignment. It's about being rooted in who you are, no matter where you are. It's about knowing that your past may have broken you—but it didn't bury you.

So whether I'm mentoring young men, building companies, or speaking on international platforms, I remind myself of that Kingston code: Walk in the middle.

Don't drift. Don't doubt. Don't disappear.

Because the middle is where everything shifts. It's where fear gets silenced.

Where manhood gets tested. Where purpose gets proven.

And for a boy from Spoilers, the middle wasn't just geography—it was prophecy.

CHAPTER FIVE

THE SEED AND THE SOIL

From the fields of Canada to the streets of Kingston—the beginning of bigger things.

Canada didn't welcome me with open arms. It greeted me with wind that sliced through my bones, skies that refused to smile, and streets covered in a kind of cold that no Caribbean blood can prepare you for. I stepped off that plane not with excitement—but with grit. Not with winter gear—but with worn- out ambition and a dream stitched together from struggle.

I didn't own a proper winter jacket. My boots weren't made for snow. I didn't even understand how frostbite worked until my toes started throbbing one morning like they were trying to scream through my socks. Every breath I took felt like I was inhaling ice. The cold here wasn't just weather—it was a test. A test of endurance. A test of identity. A test of whether my fire could outlast the freeze.

Some people arrive in Canada with glossy immigration stories— degrees, sponsors, cousins waiting at Pearson Airport with welcome signs. That wasn't me. I landed with no fanfare, just

a government contract from the Ministry of Labour folded in my jacket pocket and a heart full of war-born ambition. It was the Seasonal Agricultural Workers Program that cracked the door open. And I didn't hesitate. I kicked it wide.

Before I ever became a business owner, before I was invited

to speak on panels or mentor young men, I was a farmworker. That's the truth. That's the foundation. I was working in the cold, hands numb, body aching, sun barely rising—and still dreaming of more. There were mornings when I questioned everything. When I'd look out at endless rows of crops, knowing my back would be screaming by noon, and wonder, Is this it? But beneath that pain, there was a whisper: You're not just working for a ąaycheck. You're ąlanting a future.

You see, I had already worked for the Ministry of Labour back home in Jamaica, so I understood the system. I didn't wait for luck. I positioned myself. I studied the program, applied early, followed up, and did what most didn't: I came with intention. Some of the other men were just there to earn, send money home, and bounce. But me? I came to build. I saw beyond the season. I called every dollar I earned a seed, and I gave it an assignment. Not one dime was wasted. Every cent was either building someone I loved or buying back the future I envisioned.

When that first work season ended, I returned to Jamaica. But I came back different. I wasn't just a man who had seen Canada—I was a man who had been trained by it. I came back not just with money, but with momentum. And I wanted to multiply it.

So I did what I thought made sense: I invested in a taxi.

The industry was hot. Everybody was getting into it. I bought one outright, handed it over to my uncle, and hoped it would become passive income for the family. Boss moves, right? On paper, yes. In reality? It tanked. The money didn't flow. Every month, there was a new excuse: "The brakes went." "The driver quit." "We need a new radiator." I was managing a business from miles away, and it was managing to burn a hole in my pocket.

Eventually, I had to face the truth. The dream wasn't working. I sold the taxi. Took the loss. Walked away.

It stung. Bad.

But looking back, it was one of the most important losses of my life. Because that taxi didn't just take money from me—it taught me. It taught me that not every opportunity is your assignment. Just because everyone's doing it doesn't mean it's meant for you. Just because you can doesn't mean you should. That's when I learned the difference between activity and productivity. Between noise and motion. Between hustle and harvest.

That failed taxi business gave me my first taste of real leadership— not in success, but in surrender. In knowing when to pivot. In realizing that sometimes, loss is the soil your real future needs.

And I didn't stop planting.

Even when the first seed didn't bear fruit, I kept farming. Because I had seen enough life to know this: every seed has a season, and every season has a purpose. That taxi loss matured me. It sharpened my instincts. It helped me ask better questions. It

opened my eyes to the weight of responsibility. I didn't just want income—I wanted impact.

Those cold Canadian mornings in the field—when my breath fogged the air, when my fingers went numb from picking vegetables—they weren't glamorous. No camera crews. No applause. But they shaped me. They gave me rhythm. They taught me to rise before sunrise, to stay when others leave, to hold the vision even when the work looks invisible.

I began to see myself differently. Not just as a laborer. Not just as an immigrant. But as a builder.

That whisper inside—"This is just the beginning"—grew louder. And every risk I took after that was planted in the soil of that season.

Today, when I speak to men about entrepreneurship or hustle or purpose, I don't quote theories—I quote my life. I've touched frozen soil and still believed in harvest. I've taken Ls that felt like punches to the chest, but still stood up and said, Next time, I'll ąlant smarter. I've walked through cities where my accent made me a stranger, but my work ethic made me unforgettable.

That's why I tell people:

Don't judge your future by your current frost.

Just because it's cold now doesn't mean you're not rooted.

Just because your first seed didn't grow doesn't mean the soil's bad.

It might just mean you're still in the becoming. So plant it again.

Today, I'm grateful. Not for the frostbite—but for what it formed in me. The discipline. The devotion. The discernment.

That first visa didn't just open a door—it planted a man.

And what grew from that planting?

Vision. Voice. Victory.

Keep planting.

Your soil is still good.

Your season is still coming.

CHAPTER SIX

FROZEN TOES, HEATED VISION

Canada's cold couldn't kill the Caribbean fire.

Most people come to Canada chasing comfort. They arrive with suitcases full of hope, dreams wrapped in layers of safety, looking for streets paved with better options. Me? I came chasing purpose. I didn't pack luxury—I packed conviction. My luggage wasn't filled with winter coats—it was filled with willpower. And when you're chasing something that's bigger than your own life, comfort becomes a luxury you don't expect. Purpose doesn't need cozy. Purpose doesn't ask for convenience. Purpose walks straight into a storm with holes in its shoes and says, "Let's go."

This wasn't my first time on Canadian soil. Years earlier, I came through the Seasonal Agricultural Workers Program—swinging tools, laboring under the summer sun, every dollar earned sent home like a lifeline, each one whispering, I'm trying. Back then, I worked in faith. But that was under sunshine. That was when the ground was still warm and the sky hadn't turned against me.

This time? This time I landed in the thick of a Canadian winter.

Not a cute, postcard winter. Not the snowflake kind they show in Hallmark movies. I'm talking bitter cold. Frostbite cold. A kind of cold that laughs at your accent, mocks your courage, and dares you to quit. The wind didn't just blow—it stabbed. It wrapped itself around your bones and squeezed until your body questioned your decisions. And I stepped into that storm with **no proper jacket.**

I had been accepted into Okanagan College in Kelowna, British Columbia. The place looked like a dream—on Google. Mountain views. Clean air. Lakes that sparkled in summer. A town that looked like healing. But beauty turns cruel when your boots aren't insulated. Belief in your dream doesn't stop your fingers from going numb. And when you're standing at a frozen bus stop with frost forming on your lashes, you realize real quick— Google can't warm you.

Why Okanagan? Why not Toronto or Vancouver? Simple— **Kevin**. My bredren from Jamaica. He had come before me, scouted the territory, and sent back a word that became my anchor. "Norman," he said, "The place quiet—but trust me, you'll think clearer there. You'll build better." Sometimes that's all you need. Not a crowd. Just one voice that sees what you carry and tells you it's still worth fighting for.

Still, faith doesn't pay tuition. Faith doesn't process visas. That's where divine favor showed up, again. Back in Jamaica, a woman

at the Ministry of Labour—someone who helped process my earlier farmworker application—didn't just see paperwork when she saw me. She saw potential. When I told her I wanted to return to Canada, not as a laborer but as a student, she didn't shrug. She acted. She signed the affidavit I needed to back my study permit. She had no obligation. No family tie. But she gave me something priceless: belief backed with action.

No strings. Just favor.

When my visa got approved, it didn't just say You can study— it said You can hustle legally. I got both a study permit and a work permit. That combo? That was God saying, You won't just survive—you'll sow. But trust me—nothing in that approval letter prepared me for **that winter**.

I wasn't equipped.

No real jacket. No snow boots. No thermal gloves. Just layered hoodies, borrowed scarves, and an internal fire that refused to go out. I would walk to class with snow crunching under my feet and doubt crunching in my chest. But I kept moving. Not because it was easy. But because my why was louder than the wind.

That cold? It didn't care where I came from. It didn't respect my hustle. It didn't pause for my skin. It just kept pressing. But I didn't flinch. I had faced hunger. I had faced violence. I had faced hopelessness. So when the cold came, I looked it dead in the face and whispered, *Is that all you've got?*

While other students talked about ski trips, mountain trails, and their parents wiring rent money from overseas, I was calculating how to stretch $20 across meals, bus fare, and school supplies. I wasn't thinking about parties—I was praying for peace. I wasn't planning spring break—I was planning survival. Some students had homesickness. I had hunger—for something that couldn't be downloaded, faked, or bought.

I didn't just study in class—I studied life. I watched. I asked questions. I looked for opportunities. I refused to waste my time pretending I fit in. I knew I didn't. But I also knew—

what I carried couldn't be ignored forever.

So I worked. Any shift. Any job.

Night shifts at Walmart—stocking shelves until my knees ached.

Early mornings at Superstore—lifting boxes before the sun came up.

Afternoons at Wendy's—flipping burgers, wiping counters, managing smiles when my body was screaming.

No complaint. No ego. Just purpose in motion.

Sometimes I'd go 20 hours without real rest—bouncing from class to shift, shift to prayer, prayer to purpose. I wasn't chasing Canadian dreams—I was building a global one.

There were nights when the cold crept into my bones, even under blankets. Nights where loneliness whispered lies. But every time I thought of giving up, I'd hear that same quiet fire inside me say, This isn't *ąunishment*—it's ąreąaration.

When my toes froze, I didn't focus on the pain—I focused on

the **promise.**

Because the promise was clear:

This season will pass. But the man I'm becoming? He will last.

The winter in Kelowna didn't kill me. It clarified me. It burned away distraction.

It melted away excuses.

It carved out the kind of character that no professor can teach.

Today, when people see me in meetings, hear me speak, or witness what I've built—they see the fruit, but they don't always know the frost.

They see the polish, but not the **process**. They see the bricks, but not the blizzards.

So when someone asks, "Norman, how did you survive?" I answer honestly:

"I didn't survive—I caught fire."

CHAPTER SEVEN

THE BASEMENT F THE BREA KTHROUGH

Where most would break, he found a hidden blessing.
"Before the business, there was the basement. Before the breakthrough, there was the woman who made space."

Some breakthroughs don't come wrapped in spotlight. They don't walk in with a cheering crowd or trend on timelines. No cameras. No applause. Just the quiet thump of your own heartbeat in a place no one is watching. Sometimes, the biggest breakthroughs are born beneath ground level—wrapped in a borrowed blanket, in a stranger's basement… who turns out to

be family. That was me.

When I left Okanagan College, it wasn't just a change in schools—it was a change in atmosphere. I wasn't just relocating from British Columbia to Ontario. I was pivoting into a whole new chapter. From the crisp silence of Kelowna to the relentless rhythm of the Greater Toronto Area—GTA. I didn't have a blueprint. I didn't have a guidebook. But I had a conviction inside me, pulsing like a compass: *This is where the next chaqter begins.*

And somehow, Toronto already had a room waiting for me. Her name was Aunty Pamela.

To this day, I couldn't draw the family tree that connects us—not fully. All I know is she's from my father's side. A branch I barely climbed. But you don't always need a blood test to recognize loyalty. And that woman? She was loyalty in motion. When she heard I was relocating to Ontario for school, she didn't hesitate. No delay. No negotiation. She simply said, *"Come."*

She didn't offer me a couch. She gave me the *basement.*

Now let me be clear—this wasn't some cold, creepy space with mildew on the walls and mystery smells. This *basement* was sacred ground. It had warmth. It had light. It had quiet. It had everything I needed to rest, recover, and rebuild. She could've rented it out and made good money. But instead, she made space— for me. She chose purpose over profit. Legacy over leasing.

And I honored that gift. I didn't pay rent, but I paid in other ways. I washed dishes. I folded laundry. I kept the space clean and my presence respectful. I moved with silent gratitude, because that basement wasn't just shelter—it was strategy. That room held more than my bed. It held my blueprint.

In the upstairs hum of that home, another guardian spirit moved: **Aunty Madge.** She didn't talk much, but her actions spoke volumes. She packed my lunch. Made sure I had food for every shift, every lecture, every exam day. Some mornings, that packed meal felt like love in foil. It kept me going long after the hunger started biting. It reminded me: You're not alone.

And then there were the two pillars I didn't expect: **Bull and Sandy**—My Cousins. Bull was the kind of guy who never let you sink. When life got too serious, he stepped in with laughter, a night out, or a ride when my legs were too tired to walk. He paid my club entry like I was his younger brother—not just his cousin. He made room for me in fun, not just struggle.

Sandy? Sandy was the quiet protector. No matter what time I came home, she made sure I got there safe. She was watchful. Wise. Covered in grace and grounded in care. They weren't just relatives—they were revelation. Proof that sometimes, God hides angels in ordinary skin.

And through it all, let me be honest—**Truck Repair Hotline didn't exist yet.**

There was no business. No brand. No buzz. Just me.

A student. A worker. A Jamaican boy with God-sized dreams and barely enough bus fare to get through the week.

I juggled papers for immigration. I studied like my future depended on it—because it did. I took any job I could find. I stayed up late, filling out forms and whispering prayers that only God could hear. And yet… I never once felt alone. That house didn't just offer shelter—it offered spiritual insulation.

That basement?
It didn't **just hold me**.
It **healed me**.

Made in the GTA

Toronto wasn't easy. Life in the GTA was relentless. This wasn't small-town survival anymore—this was urban warfare. Noise. Pressure. Crowds. Competition. But I wasn't here for comfort—I was here for clarity.

I had enrolled at **Humber College,** one of the most competitive and respected schools in the country. There was no room for excuses. No one cared that I was an immigrant. No one slowed down because I had a story. I wasn't just fighting for grades—I was fighting for relevance, for dignity, for destiny.

As an international student, the pressure felt suffocating at times. Tuition wasn't cheap. Life wasn't easy. But I had one ace: **peace at home.** No matter how chaotic the lectures or how heavy the workload, I knew where I'd lay my head at night. That foundation—that basement—was my anchor.

And in that safe space, I didn't just survive. I started to **strategize**.

From the Basement to the Front Desk

The breakthrough came not in thunder—but in a phone call.

I became one of the first international students selected to work

the **front desk at Humber College.**

Now to some, that might sound minor. But trust me—it was **major**. That desk was more than a surface. It was **a statement**. It meant the school trusted me to be the first face people saw. It meant I was no longer just another immigrant—I was a gatekeeper.

Every shirt I wore to that desk was ironed with pride. Every "Good morning" was spoken with dignity. Every problem I solved was a seed I was planting in Canadian soil. That front desk became my **first platform.** And from that desk… more doors started opening.

Humber saw something in me.

I was selected to represent the school at the **Black Freedom Conference**—a historical moment dedicated to equity, truth-telling, and transformation in education. I sat in rooms I never imagined possible. Next to college presidents. Next to influential thinkers. Even near the Prime Minister.

And I sat there bold. Not because of titles.

But because I had survived the basement and now I could speak from it.

That day, I realized: I may not have a Canadian last name. I may not come from wealth. But I came with something rarer. **Resilience. Reverence. Revelation.**

I walked into that conference knowing:

I don't need privilege to speak. I just need presence.

Reflection

That basement was not the end. It was the beginning. It wasn't my prison. It was my platform.

It didn't shrink me. It shaped me.

And from that platform, I've never stopped building. Because once you realize your breakthrough doesn't need a spotlight—

You become the light.

CHAPTER EIGHT

GIVING BLOOD TO RIDE AND RISE

Shoveling snow, giving qlasma, taking buses—anything for tuition and qurqose.
"Some qeoqle gave uq after failure. I gave blood and keqt going."
"Winter didn't break me. It baqtized me into the man I was becoming."

You don't really know what sacrifice smells like until you walk out of a blood donation clinic—light-headed, chest hollow, your arm still bandaged—holding a check that barely covers half a textbook… and you still call it a blessing.

That was me.

Norman Hamilton. International student by visa. Fighter by necessity.

It was one of those semesters where everything felt like a closing wall. Tuition deadline loomed like a final verdict. I had already exhausted my options—called every number I knew, knocked on every scholarship door, wrote essays that never got read. I even reached out to people I hadn't spoken to in years, hoping

they'd see the desperation behind my dignity. But the clock kept ticking, and I was still short.

So I did what survivors do. I found a way.

I walked into that blood clinic like a man walking into battle. I didn't go there to be brave. I didn't want to be anyone's inspiration. I was broke. I was out of options. I was trying not to drown in a sea of closed doors. School wasn't just a classroom—it was my bridge to a better future. Dropping out meant losing my immigration status. Failing meant years of struggle, sacrifice, and my mother's prayers would evaporate into regret.

The nurse looked me over and asked gently, "Are you sure you

want to do this?"

I didn't answer with words—I just nodded. Because behind my silence was a storm.

She didn't know my mother was lighting candles back in Jamaica, praying every night like her son was on the edge of a cliff.

She didn't know my younger siblings looked at me like I was the one who would rewrite our family name.

She didn't know that this pint of blood wasn't just blood—it was tuition. It was hope. It was destiny being exchanged, one vein at a time.

When that bag filled and they handed me the check, I didn't waste a second. I didn't grab lunch. I didn't call anyone. I walked straight to Humber College's finance office, hands still shaking, and made a partial payment. I was still short. But I was still *in*. Still enrolled. Still standing.

I wasn't ashamed. I was alive.

And still in the fight.

A Pint for a Purpose

People glamorize sacrifice—but they don't talk about how cold your body feels after giving blood, how your vision blurs a little when you stand too fast, or how the ride home feels like a fog. That day, I learned what it means to pour yourself out—literally— for a dream.

I wasn't chasing claps or courage. I was chasing one more week in the classroom. One more opportunity to prove I belonged. I didn't feel like a hero. I felt like a hustler. And in that moment, desperation and determination danced together like brothers.

That pint bought me time. It bought me breath. And sometimes, that's all you need.

Shoveling Snow, Building Grit

You'd think one sacrifice would be enough. But Canada wasn't done testing me.

See, winter in Jamaica is a breeze. But winter in Toronto? That's war.

It doesn't care about your skin, your hustle, or your heartbreak. It just keeps falling—thick, silent, unforgiving.

I didn't have snow boots. Some days, I didn't even have gloves. Just soaked sneakers, a thin jacket, and that voice in my head that whispered, "You've been through worse. Push through."

So I started shoveling snow.

Driveways. Sidewalks. Apartment entrances.

Whatever would pay me cash on the spot. Whatever would buy me another textbook or fill my fridge with one more week of dignity.

I remember one morning—snow fell so hard, it felt like the

sky was screaming. I had a borrowed shovel in one hand, my jeans were soaked to my thighs, and my fingers were so numb I could barely grip. But I dug. One flake at a time. One driveway at a time. Because I wasn't just moving snow—I was moving shame. I was clearing a path to purpose.

Each $20 bill wasn't just money. It was proof I hadn't quit. "I didn't come this far to beg. I came to build."

The Bus Chronicles

You see the business now. You see the man I've become. But you didn't see the buses.

Before I had a company car, before I had an office or clients, I was just a man with a backpack, a bus pass, and a future worth bleeding for.

Some days, I missed my transfer and had to walk miles in snow. Other days, I lost my pass and had to choose between food and fare. I'd leave overnight shifts at Walmart, still wearing my blue

vest under my jacket, hop on the first bus, crash at a friend's for ten minutes just to wash my face, then catch two more buses to make it to Humber on time.

There were days I was so tired, I'd fall asleep standing—leaning my head against the glass of the 36 Finch like it was my bedroom wall.

Nobody clapped. Nobody noticed. But I still showed up.

And that's the thing about buses—*they don't wait.* You either catch them… or you get left.

And that's exactly how I treated life—I chased every opportunity like it was the last ride out of lack.

I Never Folded

I could've quit.

Could've called home and said, "I tried."

Nobody would've blamed me.

But I came from a line of fighters.

My mother didn't fold when the lights went out—she prayed. She didn't crumble when the fridge was empty—she fasted. And that same blood was in me.

I didn't fold because the boy who used to sell banana chips in

Kingston was still inside me—watching.

I didn't fold because I wasn't just surviving for myself—I was surviving for every kid from my neighborhood who dared to dream.

I didn't fold because God didn't drag me to Canada to let me

die in a snowstorm. So I pressed on.

Every bus stop. Every shovel. Every pint of blood. Every test paper soaked in exhaustion and late-night tears.

I pressed on.

Because every ounce of sacrifice was stitching together the man I was becoming.

Reflection

Some people quit when their bank account hits zero. I gave blood and kept going.

Some people crumble when winter comes. I got baptized in snow and came out fire.

This journey wasn't just about getting a diploma. It was about building a name.

It was about honoring every prayer whispered in Jamaican patois.

It was about rising—*even when the world exqected me to collaqse.*

"Some qeoqle gave uq after failure. I gave blood and keqt going." "Winter didn't break me. It baqtized me into the man I was becoming."

CHAPTER NINE

SET UP, STILL STANDING

Betrayed by the system. Refused to fold.
"Sometimes, God lets them fire you—because if they didn't, you would've stayed too long at a qlace that couldn't carry your future."
"Let the setuq qrovoke the startuq."

I've been fired before. It's never pretty. But this time—this time was different. It wasn't for showing up late. It wasn't for poor performance or missed deadlines. It wasn't even for a breach of policy. No. This time, I was fired for something far worse in the eyes of those who sit behind desks and call it leadership—I was fired for doing right by my family.

That kind of wound doesn't show up on your skin. It carves itself deep into the soul.

Let me take you into the scene—not as a storyteller, but as a man who lived it.

I was working at a trucking company in Canada. Day in, day out. It didn't matter if snow was falling like judgment or if my

back was screaming from the shift before—I showed up. I wore that job like armor. Not because I loved the work, but because I loved what it provided: stability, progress, proof that I was fighting my way into a future. I had dreams to fund. A family waiting on the other end of every paycheck. There was no luxury of laziness, no comfort in complaining. Just pure, raw grind.

Then came the curveball.

No warning. No soft landing. Just: "We've been acquired."

In a single sentence, everything shifted.

New owners. New agenda. New faces that didn't know my hustle, didn't care about my history.

And within days: "We won't be needing you anymore."

No severance. No handshake. No thank-you. Just silence—and then, the door.

That's what betrayal feels like. Not always loud. Sometimes, it just walks away and leaves you standing in your own loyalty like it was a mistake.

I was the same Norman. Same ethic. Same energy. But now I was unemployed.

From Employee to Chosen

But here's the part they didn't plan for.

One of the clients I had served—faithfully, with excellence, with zero shortcuts—reached out to me. No HR meeting. No corporate red tape. Just a straight call.

"Norman," he said, "Would you consider working for my company directly? I've never seen someone move like you. You bring something I want around my team."

I paused.

Not because I doubted—but because something in me cracked open.

This wasn't charity.

This was recognition.

For the first time, I wasn't just an employee with a number and a shift. I was a man whose work had made noise.

So I said yes.

I became a contractor. Not bound by a clock-in, clock-out life, but trusted to deliver on my own terms. I could breathe. I could lead. I could taste the version of freedom I had only imagined. It felt like the lift-off after years of crawling.

I was starting to see my worth not just in hours worked, but in value delivered.

Betrayed by a Bank Statement

As things picked up, I started preparing for something sacred— bringing my family over.

This was the dream. Not just success, but reunification. Not just earnings, but restoration.

I gathered documents—bank statements, invoices, deposit records—everything Immigration Canada needed to verify that I was stable, secure, and serious.

But somehow—accident or design, I still don't know—those bank statements ended up on the desk of my former employer.

The same company that had let me go.

The same people who hadn't paid attention when I carried their

business on my back.

He looked at the deposits. Saw the name of the client. The same client he'd never retained after the sale.

And just like that, something shifted.

Not one question. Not one conversation.

Just a cold accusation: "Are you working outside the comąany?"

I told the truth. I said yes.

I didn't stutter. I didn't lie. I didn't flinch.

And with no further words, I was terminated again. No due process. No fairness.

Fired—not because I failed—but because I found a way forward.

The Setup Was Also the Lift-Off

It felt like betrayal.

It was betrayal.

But what hit harder than the firing was the reason behind it. I had done everything to stay above water. I had honored the job, respected the company, never cut corners. And now, I was being penalized for surviving too well. For being resourceful. For turning rejection into resilience.

But pain has a funny way of pointing you to power.

The more I thought about it, the clearer it became—this wasn't just a blow.

It was a *birth.*

A moment of clarity so sharp it cut through every ounce of

hesitation.

I decided then: I would no longer shrink to fit someone else's container. I would no longer ask for permission to succeed.

I would build.

That moment—the sting, the silence, the slap in the face—became the exact fuel I needed to go all in.

That's when **Truck Repair Hotline Inc**. was born.

No grand opening. No media coverage.

Just a man, a laptop, and a fire that couldn't be outsourced or fired.

I didn't start with investors—I started with indignation. And that was enough.

Let Them Fire You—Then Fire Up

Some people get fired and collapse. Others get fired and *ignite*.

I didn't retreat. I recalibrated.

Because I remembered Kingston. I remembered selling snacks at school just to buy lunch. I remembered the way my mother never folded, even when life dragged her through the dirt. I remembered the boy who slept in someone else's basement but kept a journal full of blueprints.

I remembered who I was. So I lit the match.

Built the brand.

And opened the next chapter.

Now I walk into buildings I once dreamed of entering. Now I sign deals I used to only read about.

Now I hold keys—literal and symbolic—to a life I built on the bricks of every betrayal.

The truth is, every time they tried to box me out, they were unknowingly building my platform.

I wasn't fired.

I was freed.

Reflection

This wasn't just a chapter of injustice. It was the divine setup.

Sometimes, God lets them push you out—not because you failed, but because the room couldn't handle your future. Sometimes, the pink slip is permission to soar.

Sometimes, the betrayal is the beginning of the blueprint.

They fired me.

But they didn't realize… I was the fire.

"Sometimes, God lets them fire you—because if they didn't, you would've stayed too long at a qlace that couldn't carry your future." "Let the setuq qrovoke the startuq."

CHAPTER TEN

SIX GUNS AND NO FEAR

Robbed at gunqoint. Walked away unbroken.

— When life pulls six triggers, courage must answer back.

You can take my wallet. You can take my phone. But you can't take my presence. You can't take my purpose. In this life, walk bold. Walk middle-road bold.

Because the land don't remember the fearful—it remembers the fearless." — Norman Hamilton

There's a strange kind of silence that comes just before death knocks.

Not a siren. Not a scream. Not even the sharp sound of a footstep.

Just stillness. Eerie, heavy stillness. Like the world hits pause.

It's the kind of silence that presses up against your chest like a final warning, whispering: "Make ąeace, quickly."

Your heart beats like a drum against a locked door. Your spirit tightens its grip.

And in those split seconds—seconds that feel like entire lifetimes—you don't see your life in flashbacks. You feel it in questions.

What have I done? Who am I becoming?

Will I leave this street a name or a number?

That silence met me one cold Canadian evening—not in the ghettos of Kingston, but under the glow of downtown streetlamps.

It didn't come with the roar of sirens or a fistfight in the distance. It came quietly, almost respectfully, like it knew I was the kind of man who wouldn't beg.

Canada Ain't Always Cold—Sometimes It's Cruel

Canada was supposed to be the land of fresh starts. The place I came to breathe different. Build different.

It was the land where I had given my blood to study, shoveled snow just to survive, and rode buses with more grit than comfort.

It was where I believed the struggle would finally turn to stability.

But Canada ain't always polite.

It's not always Tim Hortons and smiling cashiers.

Even promised lands have shadows—and sometimes, they pull triggers.

That night, I wasn't doing anything out of the ordinary.

I had just gotten off work. Still in my uniform. Jacket zipped.

Backpack tight. Head low. No jewelry showing, no bravado, no flash.

Just a man trying to grab a few things before heading home. The kind of errand that should've taken 15 minutes and left no memory.

Instead, it became a scene I'll never forget.

“Run Everything.”

They didn’t announce themselves. They didn’t yell.

They just... materialized.

Six of them.

Faces masked. Guns drawn. No names. No warning.

One stepped forward. His voice cut through the air like cold steel.

“If you move, I will blow your head off,” he said, in a sharp Canadian accent that almost made the sentence sound polite.

But there was nothing polite about the barrel pressed into my

ribs.

Nothing gentle about the trembling metal aimed at my chest. Nothing kind about six strangers deciding, in one moment, that my life had a price.

They didn’t know who I was.

But I knew exactly who I needed to be.

I handed them everything.

My phone. My wallet. The envelope of cash I had tucked in my coat for my son’s savings. My chain.

That envelope wasn’t just money—it was meaning. It was part of a dream. Part of a plan. Part of a promise to my child that even though we were apart, I was building something for us.

And now, in a few silent seconds, it was gone.

But I Didn't Flinch

I didn't panic.

Not because I wasn't afraid—but because I had survived worse. When you've been shaped by the streets of Kingston, you know that fear doesn't keep you alive. Reading the moment does.

I stood still. I didn't try to be a hero.

I let them take what they came for—but I never let them touch my presence.

You see, there's a difference between being robbed and being reduced.

And I refused to be reduced.

They took my possessions, but not my posture.

They emptied my pockets, but they couldn't dent my purpose.

Because I don't walk with confidence in my wallet. I walk with confidence in my soul.

I'm not just carrying ID—I'm carrying identity.

So I stood tall. Calm. Collected.

Because where I'm from, panic gets you killed. But presence? Presence keeps you standing.

Sidewalks Are for Outsiders

When they disappeared into the dark like smoke, I didn't fall apart.

I didn't collapse.

I didn't sit down on the curb and replay the scene. I just inhaled. Exhaled. And walked.

And not on the sidewalk. No.

I walked in the middle of the street.

Because where I'm from, the middle of the road belongs to

those who don't shrink.

Sidewalks are for those still figuring it out.

But the middle? That's for the ones who already know.

That night, I wasn't just walking—I was declaring. Declaring that I was still here. Still moving. Still unbroken.

The world may have robbed me, but it didn't ruin me. I wasn't a victim walking home—I was a witness.

A witness to the kind of strength that doesn't scream—it just
stays standing.

The Lesson the Guns Taught Me

You'd think a robbery would leave me traumatized. But that's not what it left me with.

It left me... clearer. Sharper.

More grounded than ever.

Because something happens when you come face to face with a

weapon and don't blink.

You stop living on autopilot. You stop chasing safety.

You start walking in purpose with fire.

That night taught me I wasn't the same Norman anymore. Not the one who hustled school fees selling juice.

Not the one giving blood to finish a degree. Not the man begging for contracts.

No—I was becoming the version of me that fear couldn't touch.

I was becoming fireąroof.

Those six guns didn't take my life. They confirmed it.

They didn't end my story. They turned the page.

They walked away with a chain.

But I walked away with clarity—and the kind of focus no money can buy.

Reflection

I will never forget that moment. Not because I was robbed.

But because I realized I was ready.

Ready to lead. Ready to live bold.

Ready to face life, unarmed but undefeated.

That night, I became fearless in a whole new way. And I've been walking middle-road bold ever since.

"You can take my wallet. You can take my phone.

But you can't take my presence. You can't take my purpose. In this life, walk bold.

Walk middle-road bold.

Because the land don't remember the fearful—it remembers the fearless."

CHAPTER ElEVEN

DELAYED, NOT DENIED

East Queen Street Baptist — Where Survival Shaped My Faith

I grew up just off Queen Street in Kingston, close to East Queen Street Baptist Church, in a community many people misunderstood. Some saw struggle. Some saw limitation.

But what I experienced there was foundation.

Church was never just a building to me. It was a refuge. A classroom. A proving ground. Long before I understood my worth, it was the place where my identity quietly began to form.

5:30 A.M. — A Different Kind of Childhood

There was a season in my life when school was no longer an option.

I didn't finish in the traditional way. I had to stop early.

Not because I lacked intelligence. Not because I lacked ambition.

But because survival demanded my full attention.

Selling juice in downtown Kingston was not a hobby. It was not temporary. It was not something I tried for fun.

It was survival mode.

While other children were waking up to ironed uniforms

and packed school bags, I was rising at 5:30 a.m. to prepare bottles and head into the streets.

They were walking toward classrooms.

I was walking toward responsibility.

And sometimes—if I am honest—most times—I felt it.

Watching kids my age laughing, planning sports day, complaining about homework… living freely.

And there I was.

Selling juice.

Sometimes even to children my own age.

That feeling was real.

But I never walked with my head down.

Even in that season, I carried myself with dignity.

Because even though I was broke, I refused to believe I was less.

Talent Without a Platform

I was gifted.

Football came naturally to me. Running felt effortless.

Cricket was instinct.

I had ability—real ability.

But talent without structure is fragile. And without stable schooling, opportunity remained out of reach.

One of the quiet pains of poverty is not the absence of talent—it is the absence of access.

I often wondered what might have been if my environment had been different.

But I refused to let that question defeat me.

Instead, I reminded myself:

The world wasn't built in one day.

And I lived by a principle that carried me through:

Nothing beats a trier but a failure.

And I am not a quitter—I am a fighter.

That was not just motivation.

It was survival discipline.

The Choir That Gave Me My Voice

If the streets taught me responsibility, the church taught me confidence.

At East Queen Street Baptist, I was deeply involved in the choir.

When I stood to sing, something shifted inside me.

I was no longer the boy selling juice.

I was a voice.

I was part of something bigger.

Music gave me presence before life gave me prosperity.

It taught me how to stand tall.

How to project.

How to belong.

I liked some of the girls at church too.

But I kept my distance.

Not because I lacked feeling.

But because I felt unqualified.

In my young mind, being broke meant being unworthy. I believed I could not provide certain things, and therefore I did not deserve certain attention.

What I did not understand then was this:

Worth is not measured by what you have.

It is measured by who you are becoming.

When Education Paused — But Destiny Didn't

In the early years, I had to stop school and commit fully to hustling.

Education paused.

Responsibility did not.

But God has a way of reopening doors that life closes too soon.

Through East Queen Street Baptist Church, an opportunity emerged.

Mr. Farr, a teacher at Kingston Technical High School, saw something in me.

He did not just see a hustler.

He saw potential.

Through that connection, I was given the opportunity to attend Kingston Technical.

That moment shifted my trajectory.

It did not erase struggle.

But it redirected my path.

The Summer That Changed Direction

Another blessing followed.

Ms. Martin, a Human Resource Manager at the Ministry of Labour—also connected through the church—offered me a summer job.

That opportunity meant more than income.

It meant exposure.

Structure.

Confidence.

It was my first step into an environment that felt official—an environment that said:

"You belong here too."

From that moment forward, my life began moving uphill.

Not smoothly. Not perfectly. But upward.

Choosing to Finish

I made a decision that defined my future.

If life interrupted my education, I would restart it myself.

I worked.

I sacrificed.

And I sent myself back to school to complete my CXC.

Because I understood something powerful:

The race is not for the swift. It is for those who endure.

It is not how you start.

It is how you finish.

Every person's pathway is different.

Some begin with stability.

Others begin with struggle.

But comparison is dangerous when you do not know someone else's starting line.

I did not start ahead.

But I refused to finish behind.

A Heart That Never Hardened

Even in my lowest financial seasons, I remained loving and giving.

If someone asked for help and I had something—even my last—I gave.

Not because I had abundance.

But because I had faith.

I always put God first.

And I believe that is why, whenever life seemed to collapse around me, He made a way for me to rise again.

Every setback refined me.

Every delay strengthened me.

Every closed door redirected me.

Hardship did not harden my heart.

It deepened my faith.

Built, Not Broken

Looking back now, I do not see a boy who was less fortunate.

I see a boy under construction.

While others were in classrooms, I was building resilience.

While others studied textbooks, I studied endurance.

While others played freely, I learned responsibility.

East Queen Street Baptist Church did not just give me religion.

It gave me restoration.

It gave me mentors.

It gave me opportunity.

It gave me belief.

Stopping school did not stop my destiny.

Selling juice did not cancel my future.

Being behind did not mean I was finished.

The world was not built in one day.

And neither was I.

The early mornings-built discipline.
The missed schooling-built hunger.
The choir-built confidence.

The setbacks-built endurance. And endurance builds champions.

The race is not for the swift.
It is for those who endure to the end.

And that is how I continue to rise—

Against all odds.

CHAPTER TWEIVE

FROM BLOOD TO BRICKS: BUILT FROM NOTHING

Real estate, business, and legacy crafted from hardship, sealed with vision.

I still remember the sound of the key turning in the lock of my first home. It was quiet—unremarkable to anyone else. No trumpet. No applause. Just a man, a doorknob, and decades of struggle behind him. But for me, that moment was louder than any concert, more sacred than any sanctuary. That wasn't just real estate—it was redemption. I didn't just open a door—I opened a portal between what I survived and what I now owned.

For the first time, I wasn't entering someone else's story. I was writing mine.

That key represented more than metal. It carried memory—of every couch I'd slept on, every night I stared at the ceiling in a stranger's basement wondering, "Is this it for me?" That door didn't just separate rooms—it separated generations. I came from a lineage where homeownership wasn't even a conversation. Renting was the norm. Borrowing was expected. We learned to shrink, to squeeze, to settle. But the day I turned that key,

I broke something in the atmosphere. I shifted the story. That door didn't just open into drywall and square footage—it opened into healing, identity, and dominion. I had no rich uncle. No inheritance. Just my name, my sweat, and my unwillingness to let history dictate destiny.

But I knew one house wasn't enough. One breakthrough was only the beginning. I wasn't just trying to have a place to rest—I was trying to break a curse. Real estate became warfare. I devoured books, studied laws, asked questions others were too proud to ask. I watched YouTube tutorials with the focus of a surgeon. I spoke to brokers like I belonged in the room, even when I didn't feel like I did. I dressed one level above my account balance and asked God to meet me halfway. He always did.

In those moments of learning, growing, and studying systems I wasn't raised in, I remembered a figure from home—The Duke of Jamaica. He was a man from South Garden whose name was synonymous with respect in the real estate space. He didn't know me. Never shook my hand. But I watched him from a distance like a disciple studies a rabbi. The way he moved with quiet excellence. The way his name carried weight without noise. The way he made people believe that Black men from our community could own, not just rent. Could build, not just borrow. Could lead, not just follow. That silent mentorship planted a seed. And long before I bought my first duplex, I was already dreaming in blueprints because he modeled it was possible.

But real estate wasn't my only warzone. While one hand was learning zoning laws and property taxes, the other was building

something far more fragile: a business born not from capital— but from courage.

Truck Repair Hotline Inc. wasn't birthed in a boardroom. It was born in the basement. Not the luxury kind—the kind where pipes rattle and rent is borrowed. I had no startup funds. No angel investors. No pitch decks. Just a phone, a vision, and pressure pressing down on me like the weight of nations. It started with one question: "What if I could make life easier for truck drivers?" These were men—immigrants, fathers, brothers—who were the arteries of the economy but were treated like expendable parts. No one was organizing their repairs. No one was respecting their time. I saw the chaos and stepped in—not as a mechanic, but as a coordinator, a connector, a systems man. I became the hotline. The lifeline.

At first, the calls were few. The hours were long. The doubt was loud. But I remembered Kingston. I remembered Spoilers. I remembered how survival made me resourceful. I treated every customer like they were paying me a million, even when I was earning pennies. I built trust. Delivered excellence. Followed up when others disappeared. Slowly, the phone rang more. Truck Repair Hotline became known not for flash, but for follow- through. For integrity. For systematizing chaos.

And then came the whisper—a sense that it was time to expand.

The United States loomed large. Bigger highways. Bigger clients. Bigger headaches. But I was ready. Paperwork didn't scare me. Delays didn't distract me. I was built in fire—formed in pressure. So I gathered my faith, filed my documents, and launched **Truck Repair Hotline LLC** on American soil. That moment wasn't just an expansion. It was a prophecy fulfilled. From Jamaica's Spoilers streets to Canada's snow-choked nights to U.S. highways—I had crossed borders with nothing but God and grit. And now, I was building across nations.

But even as the business grew, I never stopped mentoring. Because I remember what it felt like to be overlooked. To feel like success was reserved for other last names. Now, I show young men how to own property. How to register their first business. How to sit at tables their fathers were never invited to. I speak—not because I love microphones—but because I carry stories in my lungs. Stories that deserve air. I speak for the mother holding two jobs with tired eyes and a dream for her children. I speak for the boy who got fired not for failing, but for being too focused. I speak because no one gave me a chance—and yet, I still rose.

When I speak, I bring it all. The blood I gave to pay tuition. The basement I prayed in. The winter nights I shivered while walking to a job I hated. The day I got robbed at gunpoint and still walked home with dignity intact. I bring the fire. The fury. The faith. Because people don't need fluff—they need evidence. They need to see what it looks like when a man builds with broken bricks and still ends up with a mansion of meaning.

And now, they call me a builder.

I build homes. I build men.

I build systems. I build nations.

But I never forget—I was built from nothing. No spotlight. No safety net. Just street smarts, stubborn belief, and divine setups dressed as setbacks. And every time I walk into a room, I don't come alone. I carry my mother's resilience. My daughter's hope. My son's future. My Woman's steady faith. I carry Spoilers. I carry struggle. I carry survival that graduated into success.

"I was built from nothing. But I refused to stay there.

Now I build homes, build qeoqle, and build nations— one risk, one word, one win at a time."

DEBTS CANCELED, NOT DESTINY

They owe me. Some of them owe me money. Some owe me credit. Some owe me loyalty, respect, time, answers. They owe me apologies they'll never say out loud. They owe me phone calls that never came. Opportunities that vanished. Support I gave freely that they never returned. I poured into people who drank from my well and walked away like they dug it themselves.

They owe me.

And for a long time, I carried that like bricks in my chest. Not because I needed revenge—but because I needed to be seen. Acknowledged. Valued. But then something shifted. I realized that waiting for people to repay what they never planned to return is a trap. A slow death wrapped in pride. I was letting old debts write my new story. And that's not who I am.

So I made a decision—not out of weakness, but out of wisdom:

I cancel the debt.

They don't owe me anymore.

Not because they paid me back. But because I paid it forward. Not because they came back to say "thank you," but because **God never stopped saying "I see you."**

Because holding grudges doesn't make me rich—it just makes me heavy. And I've got mountains to move.

I forgive them.

I forgive the ones who left when I needed them most. The ones who clapped in public and competed in private.

The ones who borrowed my time, my trust, my tools—and never returned anything but silence.

I forgive them, not because they earned it. But because I refuse

to let *them* define *me*.

My story isn't about what I lost. It's about what I survived.

It's about what I built.

It's about how I kept showing up with nothing but grit and grace in my pocket—and built a legacy anyway.

So if you're reading this and you're still holding on to the debt

someone left behind—let it go. Your destiny is not behind you.

It's not tied to who left, who lied, or who let you down.

Your future doesn't need their apology. It needs your **release.**

They owe me. But I don't owe them my peace.

I choose legacy over bitterness. Forgiveness over fame.

Freedom over payback.

Debts Canceled, Not Destiny

Because I was built from nothing. But I refused to stay there.

Now I build homes, build people, and build nations—

one risk, one word, one win at a time.

Norman Hamilton

12 TIMELESS TRUTHS BY NORMAN HAMILTON

"24 hours in a day—how you utilize it determines who you become."

"Seven times fall, seven times rise." "Nothing beats a trial but a failure."

"Give blood. Shovel snow. Miss sleep—but never give up."

"You don't need permission to be powerful. Just start walking like you belong."

"I wasn't trying to be famous. I was trying to be free."

"Every success has a sacrifice. Every rise has a rejection. Every crown has a cost."

"You can fire me, betray me, rob me—but you can't cancel what's been planted in me by God."

"I don't speak fear. I speak purpose. I speak vision. I speak survival."

"Bravery isn't always loud. Sometimes, it's just choosing to keep walking—even when you're bleeding."

"In life, walk in the middle of the road. The land doesn't honor the timid. It only remembers the bold."

"Pain is a professor. Fear is a liar. Survival is a choice."

"Every dream starts underground. Don't despise your basement— just make sure it's not your final address."

MY QUEEN, MY KIDS, MY WHY

The Woman Who Walked In, The Daughter Who Softened Me, The Son Who Carries My Name

I never grew up watching a man lead a home. I never saw real, rooted love between a father and his children. My father wasn't just emotionally absent—he was physically gone. Shot. Killed. Erased by the kind of violence that has stolen too many fathers from too many sons in places like Kingston. With his death, I lost more than a man—I lost a map. No bedtime prayers. No father-son wisdom. No blueprint on manhood, love, or legacy.

All I had was a mother who stood in the gap with both knees on the floor and both hands lifted in prayer. She didn't ask for the role of both parents, but she wore it like armor. Her strength raised me. Her faith carried me. But even she couldn't teach me how to be what I had never seen. So when fatherhood came knocking, I made a vow—silent but sacred:

This stops with me.

I became a father before I became ready. My daughter arrived in a season where everything felt fragile—my status, my income, my footing in a new country. But she didn't wait for my stability.

She arrived with purpose, not permission. Tiny fingers, wide eyes, and a quiet strength that disarmed my chaos. She didn't just call me "Dad." She called something out of me. Her love didn't make me perfect—it made me pursue wholeness. I wasn't healed, but I chose healing. I wasn't settled, but I chose structure.

And now? She's a walking miracle. A Harvard scholarship recipient. A nonprofit founder. A national representative for Canada. She's not just my daughter—she's my proof. Proof that legacy can come from broken places. That brilliance can rise from basements. That even when a father is learning on the job, love can still write a different story.

Then came 2016. Another regular day, another shift, another grind—until she walked in. Not into a store, but into my orbit. Sandinka.

She came with Marie, a co-worker I already knew. She wasn't loud. Didn't need to be. Her presence was quiet but impossible to ignore. She moved like someone who carried both storm and stillness in her bones. Her strength wasn't in words—it was in energy. It was in posture. It was in the way she made the ordinary feel sacred.

She held degrees—yes, a Bachelor's and a Master's—but what struck me most wasn't what she studied, it was how she studied people. She had a mind shaped by books and a heart formed by life. She didn't chase attention. She didn't demand to be seen. But I saw her. I saw her poise. Her clarity. Her purpose.

This wasn't someone who would orbit around me—this was someone who would walk with me. Not to save me, but to sharpen me.

Our conversations were never casual. They were catalytic. We talked about faith, family, failure, future. No fluff. No filters. And while I never needed anyone to validate my calling, I needed someone who could speak to it with reverence. She did that. Not loudly. But consistently. Not by leading the charge, but by covering the gaps.

But let it be known: I didn't become who I am because of her. I was already becoming. She didn't plant the seed—she watered it. She didn't build the man—she respected the builder. She believed in what was already moving.

When our son Norman was born, it marked more than a new chapter—it marked a generational shift. I wasn't in the room that day. I had an exam. But she didn't flinch. She delivered like the warrior she is—calm, collected, complete. No blame. No drama. Just strength. She didn't make me choose between building legacy and showing up for it—she held space for both.

Raising a son hit different. My daughter made me tender. My son made me intentional. He watches me with eyes wide open. How I talk. How I treat his mother. How I make decisions. He's not just absorbing my love—he's studying my life.

I'm not raising a boy.

I'm shaping a future husband.

A father.

A builder.

A protector.

A man who will know exactly what legacy looks like—because he saw it up close.

This chapter isn't about being rescued by love. It's about honoring the people God used to reinforce the foundation. My daughter made me evolve. My woman made me focus. My son made me anchor everything I do in legacy.

But I was already rising before anyone showed up.

Sandinka didn't create my success—she walked beside it. She didn't give me my vision—she gave it room to breathe. She didn't make me a man—I arrived as one. But she honored that man, covered him, and built with him. And that is no small thing.

So when people ask what family means to me—it's not about perfection. It's about partnership. About showing up when it's hard. I didn't come from legacy—but I'm determined to leave one.

That's what drives me every day when I look at my children.

My daughter, she isn't just brilliant—she's history in the making. A Harvard scholar. A leader. A young woman who now represents on international platforms. She runs her own nonprofit, speaks truth with boldness, and carries her name with grace. Watching her evolve into a force on her own reminds me that I wasn't just raising a child—I was preparing a powerhouse.

My son, Norman Jr., is still growing—but already, I see it. That spark. That fire. That curiosity. He doesn't just carry my name—he carries my grit. My gaze. My grounding. When I hold him, I'm not just holding a child—I'm holding the next chapter.

And I'm raising him not just with love, but with lessons. With language. With legacy.

Sandinka didn't complete me. She didn't create me. She saw me. She respected the process I was already in. She loved the man I was and stood beside the man I was still becoming.

And that's rare.

Too many people want the spotlight at the end, but she honored the shadows of the middle. She witnessed the grind without trying to rewrite the journey. She didn't build me—but she did build with me. And that distinction is important.

Because no one gets to rewrite my becoming.

I built this.

On blood. On late nights. On bent knees and whispered prayers.

And now I raise children who will walk into rooms I only dreamed of. Not because I gave them money—but because I gave them foundation. Because I gave them vision.

I often say legacy isn't what you leave for your children—it's what you leave in them.

With my daughter, I planted boldness. Vision. A voice that won't flinch in the face of power.

With my son, I've planted presence. Protection. Power under control.

And one day, when I'm not around, he'll remember not just what I said—but how I stood. How I chose integrity over applause. Vision over validation. Faith over fear.

And with Sandinka—my peace in human form—I plant gratitude daily. Because no man becomes who he was meant to be without a witness. Not a savior. Not a fan. A witness.

Someone who walks alongside the process, even when it's messy.

People often ask me, "How did you become this man?"

The honest answer is:

I chose to fight every day for what I never saw.

I chose to become the father I never had.

To build the home I never lived in.

To create the conversations I never heard growing up.

And it's not because I had the answers—

but because I refused to pass on the pain.

That's legacy.

Not just a chapter of love—but of leadership.

Not just about marriage—but about mission.

Not just about fatherhood—but about fathering forward.

When my time here is done, I want my name to echo in my children's principles, not just their paperwork. I want them to know I loved them, led them, and laid a foundation so strong, hell itself can't shake it.

This is the real wealth.

This is the real success.

And this is the man behind the mission—not perfect, not polished, but present. A man who refused to be a prisoner of his past. A man who still believes that God can take grit, grief, and ground zero—and make glory out of it.

FINAl WORD

FROM NORMAN HAMILTON

If you've made it to this page, I want to say thank you. Not just for reading—but for feeling, for relating, and for dreaming again.

This book isn't just my story. It's the sound of every underdog who refused to stay under. It's the echo of every mother's tear that became her child's motivation. It's proof that broken boys can become builders, that pain can produce purpose, and that every setback has a setup hidden inside.

I wasn't supposed to make it. Not by statistics.

Not by environment.

Not by the system's standards. But I did.

And so can you.

You don't need a perfect background to have a powerful future. You just need courage—crazy, unshakable courage to believe there's more. And if you ever forget that, flip through these pages again.

I built this book from truth, tears, and triumph. Let it be a seed in your spirit. Let it remind you that your dreams are still valid, your story is still unfolding, and your best is not behind you—it's just ahead.

Now, go build. Go rise.

Go become everything they said you couldn't be.

Because against all odds… you're still here.

And that means you're not done yet.

— Norman Hamilton

ABOUT THE AUTHOR

Norman Hamilton is not just a businessman—he's a movement. Born in St. Thomas, Jamaica, raised in the fire of Spoilers, and forged on the streets of Kingston, Norman's life is living proof that your past does not define your potential. From selling juice during gang wars to being held at gunpoint in Canada, from giving blood to pay tuition to building a life many only dream about—Norman didn't just beat the odds. He rewrote them.

Today, he stands as a proud **entrepreneur, real estate investor, author, motivational speaker, and the founder of Truck Repair Hotline LLC,** a thriving business birthed out of a basement and built on pure grit.

Through his story, *Against All Odds: The Unstoqqable Dreamer,* Norman shares the raw, unfiltered journey of a boy turned man, a struggler turned solutionist, a dreamer turned doer. Every chapter is a mirror for anyone who has ever felt counted out, cast aside, or close to giving up.

His message is simple but unshakable: **You can build from nothing. You can win, even with wounds. And you don't need perfect conditions to start—just bold conviction.**

Norman is not here to impress; he's here to **ignite**. He speaks not just with inspiration, but with **authority**—because he's lived it. His voice resonates from street corners to boardrooms, **reminding the world that purpose doesn't wait for permission.**

He is building legacy—one book, one business, one breakthrough at a time. And he's just getting started.

Let's Work

Ready to inspire your audience, empower your team, or bring

real talk to your next event?

Norman Hamilton is available for:

Speaking engagements (schools, conferences,prisons, churches, and corporate events)

Panel discussions & keynote addresses

Motivational sessions for youth, men, and entrepreneurs

Business mentorship and real estate insight talks

Whether it's a boardroom, classroom, or stage—Norman shows up with authenticity, impact, and heart.

For bookings and inquiries:
Email:againstallodds435@gmail.com

Instagram: @Iamnormanhamilton
Tiktok: @Iamnormanhamil
YouTube: Against All Odds

Website: https://authornormanhamilton.com/

Let's build something bold, together.

www.ingramcontent.com/pod-product-compliance
Lightning Source LLC
LaVergne TN
LVHW050938210926
848482LV00013B/659
* 9 7 8 1 8 0 7 0 2 6 6 4 6 *